CW00524847

SPENDING TIME WITH WALTER

SPENDING TIME
WITH WALTER

John Hartley Williams

CAPE POETRY

Published by Jonathan Cape 2001

2 4 6 8 10 9 7 5 3 1

First published in Great Britain in 2001 by
Jonathan Cape
Random House, 20 Vauxhall Bridge Road,
London SW1V 2SA

Random House Australia (Pty) Limited
20 Alfred Street, Milsons Point, Sydney,
New South Wales 2061, Australia

Random House New Zealand Limited
18 Poland Road, Glenfield,
Auckland 10, New Zealand

Random House South Africa (Pty) Limited
Endulini, 5A Jubilee Road, Parktown 2193, South Africa

The Random House Group Limited Reg. No. 954009
www.randomhouse.co.uk

A CIP catalogue record for this book
is available from the British Library

ISBN 0224061763

Papers used by Random House are natural,
recyclable products made from wood grown in sustainable forests;
the manufacturing processes conform to the environmental
regulations of the country of origin

Typeset by Palimpsest Book Production Limited,
Polmont, Stirlingshire

Printed and bound in Great Britain by
Creative Print and Design (Wales), Ebbw Vale

The examination of reality
Demands a certain unreality

Nicholas Moore

CONTENTS

I

II

III

ACKNOWLEDGEMENTS

Acknowledgements are due to the editors of the following:

BBC Radio Poetry 2000, The Devil, Poetry London, Poetry Review, Poetry Wales, Stand, Thumbscrew, Upstart!

The long poem 'The Barge' was previously published in *Agenda*.

The poem 'The Blaze' was runner-up for the Keats-Shelley Memorial Prize in 1999.

The poem 'How the First Kite Was Flown' previously flew in somewhat different form as a commission for the Salisbury Festival.

The poem 'Love and Poetry' was a commission from the Arnaut Daniel Appreciation Society.

I

SPENDING TIME WITH WALTER

At the front door, he stands apart,
his sad face in shadow. They look at me
as if to say: 'Ah. And he's with you?'
As the entertainment gathers speed, and girls
run with high-pitched laughs from one room
to the next, Walter stands in the hall.

His head is tilted back. He's looking at
pictures that ought to be upon the wall, but aren't.
From room to room, I pursue the giggling cries.
Later, I find him before an open wardrobe,
staring into mothballed darkness like a scientist.
He nods to me and we depart.

Down the drive, I remember.
My scarlet slippers have been left behind.
Returning to the house, I'm told
I may not pick them up till I've located both.
One is under the table with a girl's sandal.
I find the other. But someone's moved the first.

Standing at a pile of left-foot shoes,
I feel the glow of an obscure humiliation.
My smiling host explains: *these are for the handicapped*.
My stockinged feet are silent on the carpet,
my outdoor brogues together by the door.
On the lawn, Walter stands by a dark-leafed bush.

When I come close, he ceases to murmur.
He wears a look of Saturn. Orion blinks in his pupil.
Behind us, the house rears brokenly up
towards the moon, its lighted windows smashed.
Walter grips my arm. What could be the tie
that binds us, along the shadowed pavements, home?

If something isn't right, I don't know what it is.
Can't he speak his thoughts? At what other place
is he staring off? The distant sound reaches me
of hard, blazing music. Suddenly, he stops.
The pressure of his fingers arrests my blood.
On our faces, the lamplight makes its moves.

LONDON INCIDENT

It hadn't rained for weeks. Entering
the park, I sat beside a bowl of stone
which suddenly began to spout.
A pair of fat babies strolled by,
their pushers deep in a foreign language.
A squirrel lapped the splashes on the granite.
In a ruined jacket, on the neighbour bench,
a man was staring straight ahead . . .

From bags around his feet, he took out
green glass water bottles, one by one,
and dropped them with a crash into a bin.
The squirrel hopped away around the faucet's jet
to watch. The man became aware of us
and clinked off with his empties. I followed
his departure over yellow grass,
my gaze filmed over by the fountain.

His dapper stride looked doubtful,
somehow, through that trembling window.
Did he think he knew where real water was?
Its shabby source? In Covent Garden, later,
gypsy music seeped into the cobbled square,
and fused my blood with its lixiviating song.
The tatters of the afternoon were like ash
thickly floating down and greying up

the air. Heavy dryness shimmered,
down the sides of buildings. I put walls
between myself and the flamenco, but then
a corner one too many brought me back
in earshot of the nitre it was leaching
from the brick, its rhythm winding up
to hurl a single stick, the figure of a man,
at my frayed figure, hurrying away.

DOMESTIC

The cat slunk along the bricky line
of a wall that kept the gardens from each other,
stopping to quiz the corpse of a mouse,
then going on. It saw
the concrete roof of an old shelter, gracefully
leapt towards it, missed, and fell into the nettles.

Eight lives down, its tail curling and unfolding,
the cat emerged from weeds. Blackbirds rose
with fluttery alarums from the washing line,
as, towards a kitchen door from which cuisine smells wafted,
the cat proceeded. Ginger forepaws placed
against the door, caused the latch to slip the snib.

Fesse-wise on the lino, lay a woman,
bare beneath her morning robe, but whether young or old,
    murd'rously
deceased, or not, meant nothing to the cat. The door
swung open and it fell shadow-boxing in,
sensuously disentangling food smells from another odour,
prowled down slender limbs, sniffed human sex.

It rubbed its ear against a bruise-blotched thigh,
churring faintly, placed a clawless paw into
a triangle of reddish hair, crept beneath the silk, tiptoed on a
    still-warm abdomen,
reached what seemed to be two nesting pigeons,
and pounced on sunken nipples with a flurry
that dislodged the dressing gown. Now she was

laid open to the light. Upstairs her killer was
dismembering the bedroom, orchestrated thumps and bangs
which syncopated with the cat's
advance towards the woman's unshut mouth,
smeared a vile scarlet. Was it a mousehole?
The cat peered down the throat, past a gristled tongue, but
    nothing stirred.

Cautiously, it placed a paw upon the lower lip,
then sneezed into the mouth. Congealing
there, like golfballs lodged within
the velum, were two *quenelles de brochet*, unchewed.
A dexterous forelimb guddled for them.
Delicately, the cat began to chomp.

The murderer, descending, squinnied down the hall.
Had the tresses of her sumptuous marmalade hair
twitched upon the floor? No, it was only an animal's tail.
He'd make *pâte à choux* and then *quenelles* of the cat.
Fish and woman smell upon his fingers. Cook's knife rolled
in oilcloth. *Alors, ma petite chatte*, he murmured, closing the door.

INSTEAD OF A LETTER

In a blue sky, spring pushed out
a few small boats of cloud.
The empty lanes contained myself
and the smell of something

fresh. Then my handlebars went
snatchy over cobblestones. Dusk arrived,
the weather turned to frost.
My anorak was much too thin.

Darkness fell. I swerved
to dodge a pile of shoes, the fractured gleam
of spectacles lying in the street.
My lamp began to jitter morse.

From a bridge across a railway
I saw open wagons halted in a line.
It was freezing. And every single wagon
was crammed with people gazing up.

My flickering beam displayed
a field of suitcases, their contents
fingered by the moon.
The road bumped on and on.

I reached the vaulting gateway
of the hostel, dismounted in the yard,
received a pep talk from the thin director,
a number on my skin.

Through the night, I woke to hear
the clank of trains that never got up speed.
My room was full of odour like a fog.
I pedalled in my sleep.

The shrilling sound a whistle made,
from a far-off football field,
was endless. Though not to end a game,
it marked the end to something.

Next morning, no one was about.
In the vacancy, I felt
expectancy for my departure.
I freewheeled down an icy hill.

The sky turned back to blue again.
I got to better weather. The road turned smooth.
Cycling melds a man to his machine,
the founder says. There is no closer fit.

The letter of the month receives a prize.
I thought about it but I didn't write one.
Cycling, says the founder, gives the better sense
of what you're passing by. It's true.

THE MECHANIC

In the workshop to which I'd brought my car,
a woman in her twenties, wearing dungarees,
working in a pearl Ferrari's jaw,
heaved its motor out with chain and pulley.
The heat was such that all she wore was overalls.
Through a denim slit, I saw how thin she was,
the fragile bone and muscle under flesh.
Music roared from speakers in the shed.
An engine revved and died, then revved again.
We smiled, then someone called her name.
I started walking home and ran across a friend of mine,
back, instead of writing, from Japan,
remarking with inscrutable composure
how like Hiroshima England was,
with its windows, roofs and doors blown off.
I looked, I must confess, at everything anew –
saw the suburbs had been fractured somehow,
or someone had attempted their erasure
with means that made them much more there than not.
And as we walked together,
my friend described his wife's betrayal of him.
He'd made her tired with all his infidelities.
Inside an envelope, she'd left a lock of silken, jet-black
hair, a single, skinny, faeces curl,
then hanged herself above the garaged hulk
of his Toyota. The chattering hexameters
his sexual adventures seemed to need to be related in
(somehow he reminded me of an elastic pigeon)
slowly brought me to imagine it: the blast,
sudden thunder, louder than the mind could grasp,
a school laid open, the classroom frozen,
children turning heads to look. The end
would be, quite simply, a terrific bludgeon –

I could see that clearly. Thinking this,
I strode ahead and lost my friend,
with beating heart regained my street.
The girl was waiting, slim and flushed, beside my gate.
Her eyes were green as the ignition
of a car when you reach it through the dark.
In my living room we stripped each other bare.
I saw her haunches, bruised and oily,
where her buttock's cleft began.
She flung herself upon the couch
and held her muscly thighs apart. As we closed,
I felt her hard response,
her bolt-like tongue
riveting my neck against the air.

FROGMEN SEEKING THE CHILD
RECOVER THE UNEXPECTED

Poem beginning with a line by Shelley

Wild, pale and wonder-stricken,
the doctor foxed his lab
by climbing through the window
into the yeasty night.

Behind him, the vials,
the retorts, the cuspidors,
the brass chafing bowls,
the copper levitoons protested.

He heard
their thwarted tintinnabulation,
their angry pixie drumming.
He knew they wanted him.

Jogging through the park,
past a sprawling Venus,
a prostrate boy submitting
to a granite toad,

into the dark he ran,
toward the spires of furs
which raised their gloomy heads
around the bloodstain of the lake.

In the lab, the instruments
had gone insane.
Jittering seismically along
the bench, everything slid off,

as did he, down a steep slope —
green streaks on his white coat
which they would find later
and deduce his route —

scoring two lines deep
in the grass with his fingers,
tracks they'd refer to later
as the Pull of God.

With his arms raised
like a child to be stripped,
he plopped into the lake, to sink
beside a virgin made of bronze.

And as the pots and pans
came over the hill, no-
sing in between her rusty thighs,
he bubbled out his life.

Houses are all the same.
Sometimes it's a long corridor
that smells of whales. Now and then
you get a smiling face and a party.
Usually, the door opens
on wallpaper and walking sticks.
They've stayed at home to greet you.
Will it be alright? they ask.
They accompany you, jabbering.
I think we can fix that, you say.
They scurry back upstairs.
Cellars are where you leave people like me,
listening to the unmistakable sound
of something that goes

> *ka-slunth*
> *ka-slunth*
> *ka-slunth*

You unpack your slunth caliper, and set it up,
affix two trivets
and start the slambolica.
Once it's going nicely, the flywheel spinning, and the lightbeams
nicely intercalated
by the phased interruptor, you glimpse a figure,
snapped within the lightbeams' cross,
twisting, jumping, catching its own tail,
horny feet slapping hollow slabs . . .

> *ka-slunth*
> *ka-slunth*
> *ka-slunth*

Like someone who's discovered anguish,
you snip the blind Jeremy.
You do your Atlas holding up the world routine.
And
just as suddenly as it started
it stops.

You pack away the instruments.
You go upstairs.
Maybe they're sprawled on the living room couch.
Or they peep at you through the kitchen door.
Sometimes they're in the bathroom, splashing noisily:
the back door's open, they call.
You'd like a cup of tea, but you won't get one.
Sometimes there's a guinea on the hall plate.
I haven't seen one of those in a long time, you say.
You let yourself out.

INSTINCT

They stole my newborn child
and spirited it away. I lifted up
                    the supermarket bag
in which I'd placed it
and it was empty.

Down in the swiming pool,
they were all underwater. I had to press
                    the eardrum concussion
button
to bring them to the surface.

They floated there in masks,
nude women and men,
            with oxygen bottles
strapped to their backs, just
above their private parts.

'What have you done with my baby?
It didn't belong to you.'
            Like stones, my words
went curling out beneath the roof
and skimmed the blue-green water.

With a bubbling displacement,
a lethargic moil, the swimmers sank.
                    They overlapped
across the tiles, motionless
like carp in an aquarium.

Out of his little office
the supervisor came.
        He wore a bulky tracksuit.
His eyes were red from drinking
and his mottled hand was shaking.

'You can't stop the party,' he said.
'They've been training here for weeks.'
        'Someone's responsible,' I muttered.
'How long can they stay under?'
He shook his head.

The air stank warmly of chlorine.
I'd a big clock in my chest,
        steamed-up windows in my skull.
'I just want my baby,' I said.
The supervisor pointed.

A chubby leg
and five pink toes protruded
                from a litter basket.
She was upside down and
naked and covered in ash.

I lifted her out
and dipped her in the pool.
        'Hey, you can't do that!'
the supervisor shouted.
I dried her on my shirt.

Wrapped in my jacket,
she stirred against me.
        I walked to the exit,
and saw ten frog-masks
aimed in my direction.

THE ROWER

I worked hard for my slave status.
The advantage of my galley-chains, these shackles
which bind me to my stinking colleagues, left and right,
is that I do not even have to pretend to be civil.
One is civil whether one likes it or not, by virtue of the handcuffs
which ensure we pull together as a team, obedient to the claptrap
the galleymaster bawls at us every day.

My commitment is entirely to the progress of our vessel,
to the avoidance of troughs, Bermuda triangles, hurricanes and
    icebergs –
in other words all my former drinking companions, whom I now
    repudiate utterly
for the sake of this warm seat, the comforting sting of this lash.
I do not think about the Captain or his problems.
I have no desire to think of landfall. I suspect that what happens
    there
may involve a plank, an infortuitous disembarkation.

Imagine, with bare feet, standing on ground.
Imagine standing under trees, standing under sky.
Imagine the turn of the key in these chafed manacles,
their weight falling away. But then this oppression,
    so long accustomed to,
would become even heavier with the dread of an open heaven
lurching above me, creaking like a mast at the beginning of a gale,
and no ship to return to, only myself . . .

Somebody dies next to me. I permit myself a frown of parting
as I hear the splash when his body hits the water.
After a respite – an oath and a prayer – I feel a crack across
     my neck.
Somebody I hate with as enduring a complicity as love
screams in the prickling hairs of my ear that I am less than nothing.
With that deeply reassuring and somehow familiar constatation,
I lean forward, brace my wrists and shoulders, and begin to row.

A STORM IN THE COUNTRY

Languageless serfs
hail with raised sheep-crooks
the black cab to the overture.
Clouds put on their overcoats.

The audience is upturned clods
in a ploughed field. The weather
rattles glasses for the interval.
Scarecrows yawn in the cloakroom.

Booms. And whooshes of sunlight.
A rustic tractor wallops you
with mud from its wheels.
Lovely day, says the peasant.

The light goes out for a smoke.
Nazis bellow in the sky.
Mushrooms give seminars.
Asylum seekers button up.

Now it starts.
Percussionate downpour,
and you're the drumskin.
Be truly wet. Enjoy.

That's it.
The silence throbs with sperm.
Beetles, vipers, mice and earwigs
scuffle damply in the bushes.

There's a short coda
of something nasty
washed out
from crannied walls.

Then from rotted tree-trunks,
woodlice emerge
in glistening crowds.
A seething ovation.

THE BLAZE

Poem beginning with a line by Shelley

I was an infant when my mother went
to see an atheist burnt. The flames
reached outward from the pyre.
A voice within cried: 'No! I don't
believe in God. What's more, I don't
believe in *you*!' and sputtered into
indistinctness. A juicy gob
of something hot and liquid hit my cheek.

We munched on roasted chestnuts,
let off Chinese fireworks which made
brilliant ideograms across the blackened silk
of heaven. The vicar wore a frown.
'That's my Dad they're burning,'
said a girl my age. 'Want to walk a little?'
'Yes,' I said. I could smell her
as we tramped across the weeds into
the wood. She smelt like moonlight.
Owl dust, from a shaken wing, weighed
heavy on my lashes. 'Stand beside this tree,'
she said. 'You'll be my bridegroom.'
And then she tied me up, laid twigs
and leaves against my feet, and upright logs.
Another coil of cord went round the tree,
and spinning twice she twined herself
against me, tight. Her breath made ragged
starlight over frozen ground. I could feel
her heartbeat flicker like a bird's.
'This belonged to Dad,' she said, and stooping,
clicked a lighter on the bracken
to set us both ablaze. Through the halo

of her crackling hair, I saw her face.
'Kiss kiss,' she said. I turned and felt
the twine burn through, pulled away
and rolled in greeny ferns to douse
the flames. Her screams soared up.
Fire gripped the wood in frenzied
manacles and would not let it go.

My parents dragged me home, ad-
ministered a cuff or two, put ointment
on my seared face, told me never play
with fire and joined the vicar and
the constable to discuss affairs.
I lay in bed. Everything I'd thought about
or would in future think about, re-
played upon the shadowed ceiling.
Gently, pleasurably, I burned with first-
time headiness. My own *auto-da-fé*.

THE CEREMONY

In Neville Chamberlain's old Humber Hawk
they drove to the chapel at Mwnt.
The ring was nearly on her finger when a cry of
Dolphins! made them halt.

In their wedding best, the congregation
hastened up the cliff and looked down
at the sea's grey furrowing, lit
by the silver gleams of the sun.

Standing outlined on the edge,
tails and dresses gusting in the wind,
the celebrants saw racing shapes
suddenly break from the sound.

At least twenty they counted, jumping
in pairs. Each unisoned arc
began from the depths of a flawless
moment that happened before they could look.

Not that they hadn't seen dolphins before.
But who it was that shouted,
and *why* he had shouted, they couldn't fathom.
Time to finish what they'd started.

It was a steeper descent than climb.
The path down seemed longer.
The priest still held the ring. He placed
the warm band on her finger.

The stampede from the church
kept them worried through the sermon.
Afterwards, the lipstick on the car,
said simply: *peace in our time.*

24

Going to their window in the cliff hotel,
the bride and groom looked out
upon a sea which glittered like a sword –
unsheathed and open to the night.

They reached their hands along the sill
to touch, and waited for the marriage to begin
as if a voice might climax to a shout
in the undivided quiet of the room.

DOG

Standing on the river bank, late evening,
it felt as if the labrador were at his side. And it was
much too easy to remember passing girls
who'd dipped to fondle silky ears, looking palely
at the master, who'd smiled his secret, cruel smile.

Too easy to recall the fat man in the baseball cap
who'd piloted his pompous launch beneath the bridge,
and how the bronze-haired beauty's sudden bark
made fatty run his vessel up the bank. What friends, later,
the dog's satirical woof had won its owner!

But Corporal Schmidt — for that had been the dog's name —
was in pet cemetery. And the once-clean darkness of the water
had a covering of scum. Dusk was scummy, too, reminding him
the ruined earth he stood upon was his. That somewhere else,
another earth, where air was breathable and rivers drinkable,

must certainly exist. On that different planet,
he'd have a dog called *Scum*. They'd stroll there, too,
on paths by river banks. He'd shout into the gathering dark:
'Scum! Here Scum! Good boy! Here Scummy!'
blind to those who found the appellation odd.

Walking deeper through the evening with his dog,
as galaxies rolled into view, a horse in a paddock slept standing,
and the blueness of his home planet resembled a Chinese bowl in
    the sky,
the falling darkness would become illumination
through which he'd hear the eager kerfuffle of canine feet

as the dog came running to his call, where he knelt
on ground he could hardly see, other strollers vanished now,
its eager breath hitting him, knocking him over,
its warm tongue licking his ear, his nose, his eyes, his whole face,
engulfing him in its precipitate affection.

UNDER THE DOLMENS

hinab den Bestienschlund – Gottfried Benn

A snout broke the surface of the lake,
and on the stunted tower in the field
a man leaned into a screech of wind
that carried echoes of a cataclysmic call.
His face, a straining mask, was blind,
a blank that seemed incised from stone.

Next to him, upon the tower of stone,
a woman watched him glaring at the lake.
Had a bolt from nowhere struck him unblind?
Could he see the horror she saw, at the field's
edge, its throat agape to loose a call
of honking bestiality upon the wind?

The tower had withstood the wind
eternities and more. Its brain-thick stone
was fractured by that lewd, plutonic call.
A vast, reptilian creature from the lake
heaved across the threshold of the field.
She wished she, too, were blind.

Its popping eyes were obviously blind.
With prickling wart-hairs scanning wind,
it made a zig-zag furrow down the field
on mud-caked claws, grey as stone,
ejaculating filthy ditch-swill from the lake,
and sounding off the leaden klaxon of its call.

Epilepsy was transmitted on that call.
The man convulsed. As if no longer blind,
he ran down sixty steps and straight towards the lake,
his woman stumbling after, through the wind.
The tower toppled slowly. Blocks of stone
made giant boulder-tripods on the field.

The dripping gob-thing in the field
had magnetised the couple to its call.
Crunching them on hammer-teeth of stone,
it chewed and tossed its head in blind
devouring, then mightily passed wind,
and infamously wagged its rump into the lake.

And blind eternities came wailing down the field,
called beneath the lintels of the stone
by wind that swept them all into the lake.

WHEEL

The bus approached the plain
where the giant wheel stood.
A thin black line of people waiting
curved to the horizon.

We joined the silent queue
and shuffled over grass.
Dropping coins into the automat,
we climbed the boarding platform.

They rocked a little, as they hung there.
Dirty gondolas. The bolts slid back
and passengers came stumbling out
from cattle trucks.

We felt our stomachs lurch
as we crammed the wagon full
and felt an upward surge, that
stopped to let the next car board.

Then the wheel began its spin.
Round and round we went,
a circuit of screams and yells.
It seemed to last forever.

A noise like wind in wires,
or mournful moos of cows,
serenaded our gyrations.
Finally, we shuddered, braked.

Stilled upon the apogee,
we swung there slightly on our axle,
sensing just how high we were.
We came down, infinitely slow,

and scrambled out to where
the buses back were waiting.
The drivers grinned.
Conductors clipped our tickets.

All the long drive home
we remembered glimpses of the sky
through boarded wagon-slits,
the warmth of one another's breath,

the groaning floor beneath,
how we'd reached out once
to hold hands in the dark, and seen
the brilliance of each other's eyes.

II

THE BARGE

Handhold over handhold,
I scrabble
up the clammy sides
of my earth.
The cashbox,
prised from soft ground,
surrenders
two green-mouldy coins.
Hunger yawns in my belly.

Along the forest shore,
the river blows
on the melodeon holes
of my shoes.
Quaywards,
I do a
good-leg, gammy-leg
jog
towards the cook van,
that sags on four
half-deflated tyres
beside the water's edge.

Skulking like a dunce,
wishing nobody
the drizzling time of day,
I squeeze out quavers
from the mudharmonicas
upon my feet.
Gobs are scrunched
round dripping, grizzled,
rusty sausages.
They chew.

35

The pieman hands me down
a fat-rimmed cup.

I slurp
the scalding tea.

Kavrax passes me the nib.
Best look the man who kills you in the eye.
I scratch my fraudulent X on the paper.
Never let them know you can read.
Never let them know you can speak.
I make adversarial slashes,
I bare my neck to the sky.
Your Highness, I pray,
trash these skulls
with your majestic blows
forever . . .

Kavrax looks at me.
Can he see the Black Prince in my head?
I seem to know Kavrax's face
better than a muddy inlet
of this foul canal.
Next, he says.
I squeeze my African's tongue
and hobble away.

Name of this vessel should be
The Skeletons of Dung. Sail on, anyway,
name or no name, into oblivion.
The crew has nightmares, whimpering in the arms
of a nameless creature — our destination.
The boat's mind is me.
At journey's end, we will deliver
the slurry we have dreamed.

Hollow steps on a landing stage.
Kavrax seeks me out.
His boots stop by my right hand,
his gold teeth flash, orders
bubble up.
I go down Windy Street slumped in my jerkin,
look for the biddable Kavrax will have.
He marks them afterwards with his blade.
Never
repeat an enjoyment, he says, stroking
thighs of his sealskin trousers with bloodied cutlery,
tosses me the butt of his cigar.
I do the bidding, hear the slop
of water at the boat's prow,
listening with blank ears
to the wild laughter that cuts off suddenly
as I exhale.

Down to the Liberty Parlours,
a quick exchange of cash.
The Professor of Tattoos
turns on the machine.
The shabby canvas of my flesh
brightens with colour.
Flooded incisions. Pain.
He completes my story with a grunt.
The old lover
yearns on the curve of my right ham.
I mooch through puddles.
A fresh bride
bleeds on my left.

Kavrax's cigar smoke
breaks across the surface of his gin.
Men arrange shipments with other men.
On the tanned cheeks of my hide,
two women ride.

I wait for him to tell me
where to go, what next, which town?
The bitten nail of his right index
stabs at a chart.
In its bed, the river is stopped.

I stare
at its cold blue wriggle
in the lap of abstraction.

Kavrax clouts me.
His blow rocks
the empty sepulchre of my head.

My lovelies tighten fiercely up
in my defence.

Mornings on deck, I eat sardines.
The river moves without moving.
On the washing line
the kickless garments
of last night's copulators
shimmy.

The boy bobs up and down on the prow.

I stroke the pate
of the shrunken African head by my side,
touch my lips to its leathery,
tiny, ear.

Property of your humble servant? Thank you.
Teach your subject manners? Thank you.
Remember the gun's flash? Thank you.
Our engine parts are spread out on deck.
Courtesy of the Empire? Thank you.
Get out of my way, says Jack.

We're leaving now.
The broken-down boat
is pulled
by a broken-down horse.
We slide past yards, cranes, chimneys . . .

A man with a key: he opens a tin.
He crams the contents into his mouth, nourishes himself
on his own servility, devours
his own bidding, oil, bones, skin.
What taste! What cuisine! What hunger!

My bowels are plangent with it, the river,
its unravelling string plucking
the same note over and over
from its fretted surface.
Rain – or is it sleet? –
pesters my knitted cap.
A fellow in black, some innocent,
stands on a bridge,
twisting his hands in his face.
I stare up as one would
at a perpetual suicide.

Later, I raise
the skull of my African
to the level of my gaze.
With a fractured grin,
it faces the moment
of eternal severity.

The palm wine
you offered them, I whisper,
they tipped out, laughing,
upon the earth . . .

Kavrax hits me, I stumble,
the body of the water takes our weight.

This is the stain
my tongue licks up . . .

The river eddies
in my blood.

We glide
through folds of filthy fog.
The boy calls,
naked, from the prow.
He has a white voice.
The world is a lost echo.

On the muffled clatter
of a moped,
an invisible man rides the towpath,
nakedly seeking
a place to fish.

Soup on the stove.
I do my patient shuffledance
around the pot
as the vessel bumps the banks.
Jack, the mechanic, steadies himself . . .
Pea soup, he says laconically,
holding a plate.
I heave the ladle.
We sink deeper
into the diseased brume.

The diesel goes dumb.
From the rubbed-out river banks,
I hear the cough,
of birthday-suited anglers.
More soup, says Jack.

He slurps it down
and climbs the galley steps,
off into the murk.
I know he's out there,
shoving the oilcan spout
against the nipple of a greaser.

Jack's the man.

A nude embracing a machine.

We're moored.
A cloud of prayer issues from the church.
Dry lips move in unison.
Two officials and the Chief of Police
move in step along the street.

Kavrax, in the stern,
frowns across the jetty.
He gives me a bag.
Full of prayer books, he says.
Prayer books with pictures.
The kind that make grown men sweat –
little think-pictures to run the tongue across.
Get rid of the bag! says Kavrax.
With a shovel under my left elbow,
a bag in the crook of my right,
under a dismembered tree,
in a forgotten clearing,
I stand, remembering . . .
Don't tell me where
and don't try to remember where
you bury it.

With a sharp spade,
the rusty hinge of held breath scraping,
I open the lid of ground,
crumbs of soil running back,
the bag dropped in and covered.
Lose memory now.
See the river, go left.
OK feet, now another direction, then straight line, left again.
Lose it properly.

Forget the lie of the land.

Right?

Out on deck.
November sunshine.
A heron.

I dip
down into the laundry
and up again to peg it out.

A moan from Kavrax's cabin.
The door's ajar on a girl.
Her eyes light on me, light away,
sex still open as if she cannot close it,
stink of cigar turning to frowst.
I'm off.
Brass to polish. Dishes to do.
At the galley sink
the clock's tick makes silence longer.

Above me, his steel dancers
kick this way and that.
The boat rolls, and I
take a step forward, take a step back.

A cough or something.
A sniff.
She points to
the mark
cut in the rind of her thigh,
fattens herself
by the doorjamb, watching me.
I point
to those high kickers . . .

                    See
the hooks they hang upon —
his knives?

45

Hours pass
in the cold seclusion
of the water,
under a low sky,
between the banks
of concrete and grass
through which we move.

Then mornings pass
and evenings.
Then days.
The ropes coiled up on deck
are uncoiled
and coiled up again.
Someone rides the bicycle
stacked in the stern.
Coming upstream, other
boats move steadily back
into the time
from which we came.
Leaning on the rail,
men watch them.

In the unreadable movement
of motion pressed
against its weightless counterpart
everything
is quite still . . .

The boy squats on his bunk,
a thin, brown leg swinging . . .

When we anchor, men arrive,
query him, his undone shirt buttons,
run their fingers over his ribs, and smile.
Kavrax nods. He clips his cigar.

We travel, the boy and I,
between warehouses, into a town.
His lonely face
wears the look of an angel.
I stand over him,
guarding the anxiety I see
in his readied eyes.

Terminus, the end of safety.
Hand on the scruff of his neck,
I walk him
down the empty alley,
knock at the tavern's back door.
They take him upstairs.
I stand at the bar.
A shape slithers towards me
over the loose boards of nowhere.
They bring him back in, handing me the envelope.
Through the furnace-mouth of the door
we stumble.
The tram runs through cobbled streets
towards the port. The distant smell
of the river is a cold blindness
of the heart. On his shoulder
the flame of my hand

steadily burns. Buttons torn off, I notice.
Walk upright, I hiss. *Try not to fall.*
Think where I put the needle and thread
to repair that shirt. Then the lights
of anchored craft,
tethered to rusty oildrums,
riding the spew
of the town's cess.

On the riot mattress of no sleep,
the boy turns feverishly in his bunk.
I take out the skull of the Black Prince,
perch it on the headboard.
Eat the breath of his enemies, I whisper.
From a half-dream, the boy looks at me.
Heat in the tripes of this ship,
great heat. It makes the walls glow,
the nailed furniture. The slop
of fiery water against the hull
drips
on the icy plate of my brain.
Naked, he has twisted the bedclothes to a stranglehold.
His eyes hold me as if
to dismantle me.

The ruins
of the darkness whisper.

From the deck, I watch
a lighted inn
blaze through the dusk.
Below me,
men talk softly and conspire,
lie in their bunks,
stare at the ceiling
that moves with them.

Progress grows out of nothing,
an illusion of water and grey trees.
A single crow creaks over ploughland.
A car halts
by a darkening wood,
extinguishing all lights . . .

Our boat's furrow
is an incision
deep into the stream.
It opens the hearts
of inert carp, ataxic pike.
A thin trail of black blood
curdles behind us.
The moon silvers it.

Progress grows from the river,
shabby as froth.

The barge grates
against a rotting wharf.
Kavrax, with clipboard,
ticks frantically,
motions me to come.
I look into his face
and he looks back.
Nothing.
We drive
in a silent car
through street after street.
I look up and see
fantastic sculptures
on a great building.
Men dancing
in a ring.

I crouch
with my back to a marbled wall.
Electric doors flow open.
From the fast elevator, Kavrax
tosses me a leather bag.
The doors whine shut.
He rides to the top.

I open the drawstring.
Beads of glass roll out and down
my legging-folds.
At the reception desk, they peer,
scrutinise me closely.
Kavrax carries
bills of lading, freight documents.
From each bead of glass
a miniature human face
looks back at me.
I squat, convulsing, in the centre
of a paralysed ripple,
vomiting shadows
on the dark pool of the floor.

The marbles run riot in my lap.

On the twenty-fifth,
Kavrax stands like the boss he is.
He holds out his hand
for the greeting
that will clinch everything.
I think of wagons departing,
goods radiating outwards in my head,
employees unscrumpling documents,
reading them again and again,
disbelieving
the consignment . . .

I put back
each trapped stare in its bag,
tighten the neck, make
a feverish inventory of all my head contains.

At midday, men perch
high everywhere in cold sunshine,
silently watching.
Cranes swing.
Wagons screech
on glinting rails.

A limousine
slides to a halt
– box coats and clacky shoes –
the friends of Kavrax.
They group on the harbour
and a sheer note
rises through their laughter –
like someone
wielding a knife for a dare.

They lift
invisible glasses,
a toast
to the high-stacked boxes.
I stare at the man
in the cabin of his crane,
building with each swung pallet
a skyscraper of delirium.

Steadily

the hook winches

downward.

We are
on the deck of a bedlam ship,
driven nowhere
by dieselling mouths.
The boy, with a weak smile, soft in the head,
holds a glass and stares round the next bend
with curved eyes.

More booze!

Kavrax laughs.
In the bar of the *Trumpet and Jericho*,
hilarity sows
the panic of its own loudness.
Drink up! he shouts.
I stumble to the door, out into the cold.
On the frozen slabs of the quay,
I stand by the water's edge, the racket
of thoughts gummed on my face.
A noiseless frost is everywhere.
Above me, in lighted rooms,
men apply the rule of thumb
to this shadow under a tarpaulin,
our country, this shipment
that has to be assessed.
Invaded, I reel
through the dark. Somewhere different
tries to get into my head –
where parrots flutter,
monkeys groom each other,
and warm rain falls on a forest.

Underneath my feet,
the icy flagstones
crunch.

Against the current,
the diesel has a deep, booming note.
Hull high in the water,
we bore upstream.

I imagine the Black Prince,
his malicious gift to a rival:
a married woman.

She welcomes
the new lover
into the darkness of her arms . . .

The moment of pleasure.

Then
his adulterous skull
is cracked
from behind.

Cleaved to the kitchen slate,
I crouch on the stool,
making soup, scraping carrots,
dicing and chopping, fast and sure.

No gifts for me.

I'm barefoot,
dodging rabbit-holes
across the plains of Africa.

At night, I brood
on shipments to come.

There'll be a next time.
And then another next time.

Still dreaming,
I dream the forest,
beneath a hush of branches.

When the owl
beats slowly
through the wood,
I take out my catapult,
pull back the unloaded sling
and let fly
an invisible stone.

The owl
whirrs on
between the trees,
its infra-red eye
scouring the earth for prey.

An owl . . . ?

Beyond the trees
the land opens out flat.

The mice are running.

At dawn we tie up.
Men of property alight from taxis.
Listen to me. Listen to me. Listen to me.
Disbelieved girls sob to the tribunal.
Wait here. Move there. Sign here.
Delivered. Delivered. Delivered.

★

Kavrax staunches,
with coins pressed hard into my palm,
the wound that returns
all the way down
the canal of my nerves
to its source.

And smiles.

★

Along the river shore,
a loose sole
flaps a counterbeat
to the hobble of my gait.
New shoes now. New shoes now. New shoes now.

The wind sweeps clouds
against the sky's blade.

At the door of my earth
I turn back the grass.
Finger over finger, I
scrabble down the sides,
dislodging gobs of soil
deep
into the burrow's warmth . . .

Freedom!

III

LOVE AND POETRY

en cest sonet coind 'e leri

after Arnaut Daniel

Here's a poem, nervy, graceful,
made from language shaped and smoothed,
assembled like a cabinet and glued.
I'll give each word a rasping glance
of my joiner's file until it dove-
tails with the next, and I've a song
that won't betray my inspiration.

Every day I'm less disgraceful.
She's the one who has improved me.
Take this metred peek into
a heart perfected by her radiance
and see how good I have become.
When winter hurls down rain in clods,
I receive a love-libation.

In the flickering cathedral,
let candles burn so I don't lose her,
and let my crafty service prove
that verse can win what effort can't.
Watch the way her gold hair tumbles,
riding out to test the crop.
No Lucerne beats that sensation.

Desire arrests me in my chamber.
A man who loves like me is doomed
to strike a match and watch its lucent
flame go wild. She's advanced me
all the gift of her existence, and I'm engulfed.
Usurer, she owns me, forge and workshop.
My soul's a crackling conflagration.

Not even empires could replace her.
As Pope, I'd have to excommunicate her –
but rank is just an insult to my mood.
With the arrow of her beauty in my heart,
I'll feel the quiver of her tongue
upon my mouth before the year has gone,
or I'm a corpse, and she's damnation.

Renounce her poet, no, you mayn't –
have her, not that either, fool . . .
Scribbling in this darkened room,
I hammer rhymes into their harness.
Love's more hurtful than to trudge
behind a plough. My bitter lot
is Moncli's for his Audiart – frustration.

Call me Arnaut. Against the flood,
I swim (what else?), chase hares upon an ox,
and clasp the wind to my embrace.

IN WHICH HE IMAGINES HIS BELOVED
IS A FLOATING RESTAURANT

My twin-funnelled riverboat, my love,
I miss the slow-accelerating crunch
as your paddlewheel begins to turn –
all you offer me is lunch.

You're moored so fast to shore,
it's hard to think that you
were once a navy's pride,
bearing southward with a crew.

Let me come aboard, let me
enjoy the groan you make
as I displace you, feel you settle
to the sly command I take.

Pistons seized in sludge,
smokestacks dead to puff –
how long since someone stoked
your furnace, made you chuff?

I'll stroll the deck of you,
stroke your polished side,
caress the workmanship of you,
catch the rising tide.

Not yet, not yet.
We won't cast off,
till every rivet, every weld-seam's
threatening to pop.

Then, with moony, charged velocity,
we'll hoot a hornpipe to forewarn
the villages. Our honks'll join
the bird calls of the dawn.

My cries will be like rain upon
your spray-whipped bridge.
In the estuary, we'll
fathom every crest and ridge.

And out to sea, my fingers
tangled in your rigging, we'll steer
away from land, into the great
Atlantic's roll, and disappear.

AUGUST

I

The cricket does its intermittent washboard scrub.
A lorry whines along the curveway of the dike.
Market day, but the orchard leaves are still.
In the linden tree, a chaffinch pipes sporadically.
Under an August sky, the old take overheated steps.

II

The boys in the pool — did I hear this right? — are playing *editors*?
The car behind is being driven by a psychopath.
The news is full of the delinquencies of Presidents.
At every Imperial stiffening, the Dow Jones falls.
Under an August sky, the shameless are making themselves known.

III

I will turn down the offer of a huge amount of money.
I will take a job in the supermarket in order to be close to her.
Henceforth, I shall burn every book once I have read it.
I will discover a buried talent in myself.
Under an August moon, her hair will darken my pillow.

THE VIEW FROM BIRD ROCK

An adder fissured through the brown grass.
A single gull cruised to the undercliff.
Our glasses swept the waves
as if from the bridge of a vessel.

That morning we'd seen
pictures of the man who'd left
his dead wife on the bed in the hotel,
and cut his visit short.

Now, thoughtfully, we waited
for a dolphin to thrash high, to jack-knife,
glittering, to re-enter the water
smoothly as a key.

No dolphins at all.
Hoods of anoraks pulled up, we looked
into each other's patient faces
and at the sea.

Down there on dolphin boulevard,
shadowy creatures
swam through rippling pilasters,
where finny women lounged

and heavy-torsoed men
idly flexed and eased.
White teeth flashed
through beards of bladderwrack.

Each soft, pendulous, female
earlobe invited a nip. Each sea-grey male gaze
appraised heavy thighs, arching
bellies, webbed feet.

The ocean boomed. We seemed
to hear demonic deep fidelity
being sworn in language
not by any means describable in ours.

The afternoon stayed featureless.
Cloud broke up and formed again,
every moment crammed to bursting
with a hurried vacancy.

The tides of dusk rolled in. Wave-tops
posed for snapshots, dissolving into smudge.
Back we went beneath a sky
reeling in a catch of early stars.

He was there again, grinning on the TV
in the lounge. Said he'd woken up
to find her dead was all. The holiday was over.
So he'd gone home.

THE STINK OF THE TROUBADOUR

Life was my sirventes.
Garlic the sword on my tongue.
Anger filled the sails of my verses
and blew them into port
where they held the WELCOME sign up
backwards to EMOCLEW me.

I exhaled a poem or two to clean the air.

They brought me in beneath the harbour walls,
a town of half-intrigued, recoiling matrons,
and clapped me in a tower.
I'd evil-mouthed the baron
and much-too-fondly-mouthed the baroness.
The gusto was to blame.
My cell was slightly longer than its door,
but wide from narrow windows
I threw the garlic, knotted in escape sheets,
dangled it
disgorging feculence like rowel-spurs
against the flanks of self-admiring stone.
Knobby cloves, hold fast, I thought,
spring me from this castle
much too high with handsomeness,
and then, my friends,
I swarmed on down those strings
of lumpy toothsomeness
and off I went across the fields.

The village girls turned pale.

In market places up and down the land,
I hummed my way past onion-sellers,
fondled crisp provincial globes, and stole
a dialect as pungent as the local cheese.
Let your nose be ears, I thought,
to catch this high-toned lilt of mine.
Let your brains be teeth
to chew upon these bitter-flooding
bulbs of spleen. And pass
this mouth-impugning music on,
gustily into a loved one's face —
my breath, my language and my song.

CREATIVE WRITING

Humbled by the need to earn money,
made haughty, I confess, by the dim talent of my pupils,
I brought a dead frog to class and bade them
consider it attentively for twenty minutes,
preparatory to writing a poem they would call 'The Dead Frog'.
After three minutes of whispering a chair cracked back.
Its owner stood tensely, squaring off against me.
Then another leapt to his feet in a splendid show of recalcitrance.
'You haven't seen it yet,' I told them, and walked around the table,
gripped the smaller of the two, kneed him in the back
and smashed his head upon the table of polished oak.

I bound him with rope to the chair and instructed the class
to consider him attentively for twenty minutes
preparatory to writing a poem they would call 'How the
    Unconscious Works'.
Then I ascended to my room, took pen and paper
and knew with thrilling deliberation that soon I would have
    a poem.
Downstairs I could hear voices and the shifting of furniture.
As feet began to climb the stairs, I scribbled faster.

ONE WORLD BOOKS

In Memoriam

The bookshop is gone now, where I once bought translations of
  Edmond Jabès,
the letters of William Carlos Williams to his publisher and a
  biography of Robert Graves
which purported to tell the truth about Laura Riding. It has been
replaced by a JOPP! sun-parlour, that is to say a place
where people recline nude upon glass beds while a brilliant
  counterpane
lowers itself with a whirr to within inches of their exposed navels
and proceeds to bombard them with iridescent rays which may or
  may not be harmful
but will have the certain effect of rendering their skin rubicund, not
  to say, leather-coloured,
and make them look healthy to the outside world, no matter what
cankers lurk in their brains. Thus it is, say,
that thirteen-year-old girls will prostrate themselves before Old
  Father Sunlamp
in exactly the same spot where previously Hölderlin and Goethe
  were displayed,
and equally nude middle-aged men will lie dreaming
of thirteen-year-old girls stretched out compliantly beneath them
where once the many remaindered publications of Middle-western
  universities,
dealing with problems of structure in language, aesthetics
and 'the unreadable poem', in prose as numinous as it was obscure,
were piled in bargain discount profusion for the eager intellectual
  browser.
Or, but this is quite another scenario, those former browsers
  passing by,
angry and saddened at the thought of intellectual humankind
now reduced to the status of the filling in an illuminated sandwich,

will suddenly fume with a profound and ethically-inspired
    indignation
while remembering a sentence such as this: *'We must now
    abandon the idea*
*that a poem is a window onto the truth, we must evict the
    "deeply-sensing I"*
who examines its soul for the benefit of its deeply-sensing readers
and substitute the multi-layered, coming-at-you-from-all-angles gabble
which is the inescapably witless kernel of all communication . . .'
And, oho, think the former browsers, well, how right it is that
    bookshop has been demolished,
how appropriate it is those would-be readers now lie stacked,
like the illustrious dead, in prone coffins of luminescence,
absorbing electrical discharges for as long as their coins hold out,
NOT dreaming with closed eyes of aesthetics or life's wee
    epiphanies,
NOT swooned upon a bright beach of glass, grieving for the
    absence of literature,
but lying there, simply, trapped between abysmal hummings of
    the bulbs,
like butter-coloured lotos-eaters spinning to withdrawal,
until with a snap their cabin goes dark and the top half of their
    radioactive bun
pulls slowly away, leaving them to glow faintly and ludicrously
in the darkness through which they must now stumble to find their
    clothes . . .

THE COMPETITION POEM

kept all its hats on
was little feet running down a corridor very fast, little feet,
    goodbye, goodbye, very fast, pitter pat, aah!
took two years for every comma OF WHICH THERE WERE
    TOO MANY
paid five quid per entry
rhymed, so it won
resembled a home appliance, immaculate, white and cuboid
was about a taxidermist
was terribly descriptive
was about a child discovering how beautiful a lie can be
was included in the Pope's last anthology
shot itself in an attic and missed
encountered leprechauns on Parnassus, spoke to them, and O
    gruffly they answered back and the poem wrote it all down
ran out into the street with no clothes on, howling FUCK ME!!
lay calmly in the path of advancing theorists
fainted at the mention of mirth
said it was a mural really, in need of a wall
rose beaming like an organist into the Odeon of life
dipped its polished brogues gingerly in meaning
asked the committee if they would like to see its laurel wreath
hinted it had danced on Olympus with Sheila Maelstrom
sent a friend to the postbox, being superstitious
was disqualified later for failing to sign the cheque

HOW THE FIRST KITE WAS FLOWN

I didn't have a name for it,
although a *kite*, I thought, might be a way
to render visible what we fearfully
divine — a sort of heavenography.

On the ever-arching page of sky,
I loosed a long-tailed quill —
utensil of transcription and research —
to read what it might scribble.

Taking down the wind's dictation —
mandarin decipherer of every
dashed-off, gust-shaped ideogram —
I held the swooping line.

I must have looked an idiot,
trying to restrain that cursive,
twirling on a single blowy spot,
my cloak tied up in knots.

Behind my cuneiform moustache,
I think my face was pale.
I may have seemed ridiculous.
Does seem mean *be* ridiculous?

Two girls with eager glances,
and their mother in silken green,
a dragon around her waist,
followed the creed of my wrist.

I saw the levity of their delight
at what I did with gravity,
and looped my freehand fiercer
on heaven's airy blank —

a plumb-line hurled at nothing,
measuring its depths,
calligraphic poems that vanished,
illegibly, beyond redress . . .

HOŞ GELDINIZ

The guide book says:
a stamp from the north in your passport
will mean you cannot be admitted to the south.
Have your visa entry stamp, therefore,
on a separate sheet of paper.
'*Hoş geldiniz*,' says the barber.

From the barber's chair, a voice translates:
'He means welcome. Will you drink
coffee?' A woman, smiling, brings it.
'For thirty-five years, I lived in Palmer's Green.
I am a taxi driver,' says the man to the mirror.
'Now I spend winters on Cyprus.'

Parked under a lemon tree in town
is a street cleaner's cart. The tree suddenly shakes.
A ragged man and a hundred bouncing lemons
descend. Then it begins to rain –
water flows swiftly down deep culverts and out
into the orange groves of Güzelyurt.

To a group of German tourists, Mehmet explains:
'Here we have British sockets. However
by inserting a matchstick into the earthing slot,
you can use them for the two pin plugs you have.'
Later, as the tour bus navigates an oil-drum check point,
one of them says: 'You Turks are too hot-blooded.'

Mehmet laughs. It's the kind of laugh
that betrays a familiarity with prejudice
he knows he mustn't let bother him.
Despite himself, he suddenly looks grave.
'*Ich will nicht politisieren,*' says the German.
'*Ich will nicht politisieren.*'

In The Green Jacket bookshop,
The Cyprus Triangle by Denktash is on sale.
Thus are the armed soldiers explained, as they smile,
hold up the car and beg a lift, winningly, to the next village.
Beside the stunning azure of the sea,
is asphodel, that greeny flower.

Men sit out on the pavements of Lefkosa. Small cups
of coffee are carried to them in trays on chains.
It isn't Islam that has banished McDonald's.
The Green Line is a tumble-down wall which stays up.
'Two weeks and no ice cream,' grumbles a hotel guest.
Through a slit, someone watches you.

Below St Hilarion, in Bellapais,
like silence by music,
the hush is broken by whispering luxuriance
of leaves. Playing backgammon,
the men and boys tilt their kitchen chairs forward
in a corner made of Gothic stillness and ruins.

Wild cyclamen, blue anchusa, and the yellow
of Bermuda buttercup. From Vouni, you could imagine
the Argonauts might come sailing round a cliff.
An ancient signboard in Lefke
says *Shirts cleaned and collars starched*.
'You get a better deal here,' the UN soldier remarks.

'If Denktash makes a deal,' says Mehmet,
'I take my family, go back to England.' Offered a drink,
his face wobbles in horror. 'No, no.'
A great Turkish flag is cut into the side of Beşparmak,
and Ataturk walks the heights, smoking his pipe.
'That's what started the fires we had last year,' says Mehmet.

When the plane lifts off for Istanbul,
you realise the gestureless, effaced idea
of going somewhere for the weather
has unravelled in a welcome
steadier than sunshine. *Hoş bulduk.*
Good that we have found each other.

THE SANIBEL STOOP

The osprey defecated
a virulent, slashing stream
into the blue swimming pool,
and screeched from a nearby palm.

In the irritated wind,
fronds scraped down the edge of air.
A green hosepipe lay coiled up.
Distantly a screen door banged.

A white pelican swept fast
across the sea, its wingspan
tipped with black. It glid an inch
above the waveless back bay,

lifting up to cross a dock,
then down, onward, out of sight,
its beak thrust forward, a
prehistoric aviatrix.

Out to sea, a storm would be
bringing in the shell harvest.
I walked the lane's length, keeping
my ear tuned for a hallo.

Everyone had suddenly
gone, except the cormorants,
spreading their wings out to dry.
From nowhere, clouds were coming.

Stood by a breeze-ruffled pool,
a white egret observed me.
Its beak clacked emptily twice.
It sounded like that screen door.

Now the shells would be rolling,
driven hard through the high surf
in sea-dark, tumbling masses,
snatched at by the undertow.

I imagined tomorrow:
Fighting conch. Periwinkle.
Giant calico scallop.
Shark's eye moon and sand dollar.

Fiercely gathering the shells,
I'd stoop and thank the power
that held the sea's jaws open.
It would feel like getting rich.

EPIPHANY

We sipped our Rioja and discussed
the strange figure under the lamppost outside.
Christmas was officially over.
Pippa said that black policemen in Brixton
were being painted white
and Chris explained that the Welsh
were frozen but nice. We had had a good meal, though I
had committed a serious *faux pas*,
having taken a salad bowl of lettuce
intended for the whole company
to be my portion. Then we adjourned
to the sitting room, carrying
what was left of our drinks. Our host
left briefly and returned, smiling, with an axe.
Hesitantly, I asked for another glass,
but the wine, though it had not run out,
turned out to be in an unreachable room.
We began to discuss Bosnia
as our host pricked balloons on the tree
with a champagne cork clip, making
a series of fearful pops.
Hatty asked if we could define *angst*.
Our host removed the silver tresses
from each branch of the tree
and scrumpled them into a ball.
I asked him whether
it went against the spirit of the thing
to save the tinsel for another
Xmas. Our host, for answer, tore
the fairy from its pinnacle and hurled
it into the fire. We mulled
self-consciously upon our empty glasses.
Jo said Yorkshire was closer

than you might think. Matthew mused
upon the freshness of that angle.
Then our host stood up and grasped the axe.
The room resounded to its thuds
against the bark. Needles shivered
into the laps of the guests, and we all
rose nervously from our chairs,
making way for the tree, as it toppled and fell.

OLYGOPTL

My mother was a German.
She parachuted down over the north in 1939 –
single scout of the advance Lake District shock wave
for an invasion that failed to follow –
and married my father instead.
My father was French. '*Bonjour, mon fils,*' he'd say,
at breakfast, inviting me to share his cheese.
He carried onions slung across the crossbar of his Raleigh.
When he lectured his assembled staff, his waistcoat pockets
would reveal the tips of cigars, poking out like rockets.
At home we had a Maginot line
which was me.

In our house, therefore, we had a mini-European Union,
long before anyone had thought of such a thing.
By marrying a Frenchman and renovating the kitchen, my mother
    felt she exhibited discernment.
My father was of the opinion that home improvements were
    eyewash.
He read Proust, Valéry and Mallarmé and would quote freely
    therefrom.
'Zere is no realitee,' my father would say, 'except ze words in your
    mouth.'

Like many Frenchmen, my father was an authoritarian papa.
I was imprisoned in the boot cupboard for smoking and wearing
    my mother's bra,
and on one occasion he caught me uncorking my first claret
and struck at me with his freckled fist. '*Nom de Dieu!*' he
    thundered.
My mother put herself between us and was laid out cold as a carrot.
'*Regardes ce que tu as fait!*' cried my father.
'*Du hast mir Weh getan,*' cried my mother.

'You've gorn and dunnit naow, Dad,' I said.
Later that evening my father quoted his favourite line from
   Mallarmé,
'Je suis triste, hélàs, et j'ai lu tous les livres.'
My two brothers were encouraged to speak first the King's English,
   then the Queen's,
and many were the regal conversations we had over the roast lamb.
My mother worshipped nature. I mowed the lawn.
My father never did the washing up or ironed a shirt.
It was Deutsche Romantik versus La France Profonde.

When they went out to the cinema,
I'd lie in bed and dream the film they saw.

THE MACHINE

Poem in five sentences

Of course the operation of chance makes us sad –
it's a mechanism of such intricacy, such febrile, whizzing purpose,
undoing logic, pulling rugs from under feet
with gossamer claws that grab and whisk away
the carpets, those who stand upon them, and vanish everything
so swiftly into the black hole of fate, that frankly
you feel disappointed and then annoyed and then quite melancholy
that life should contain such expeditious little grabbers,
not to mention the mill-wheels of crunching Derbyshire stone
between which everything is judiciously pulverised before being
blown into the atmosphere to become the stars
you stand there ruefully gazing up at
from the temporarily too-solid ground.

This juggernaut was invented by a Frenchman,
by name Jacques Le Sourd
(or Jack the Deaf, as we would say in English),
whom an English farmer, feeling rightly
that leaving chance to chance was much too chancy,
hired to build an Engine of Good Fortune
in what had once been an orchard of Cox's Spiffins, causing
their genetic stock to be erased completely
when foundations were laid down for the device.

Horse-drawn wagons
brought the milled parts from Sheffield, Leeds and York, although
Le Sourd was killed by the falling spanner of a workman, leaving
his hopeful blueprints for one Hamish McPosset
to get inevitably wrong and therefore build
the grinding factory of doom we know today which
necessitated Egyptian-pyramid-style building methods until

the great flywheel, all 300 tons of it, was started up,
with a clicking of sprockets, a chattering of pulleys, re-
distributing luck, hazard and confusion on the basis
of no basis at all, so that
as the slowly accelerating thump of its mighty pistons
began to eliminate with fuzzy precision all the previously laid plans
of mice and men, Hamish McPosset himself, whilst walking
with the excessive caution one would expect of a Chance Engineer,
on a high gantry beneath the corrugated iron roof, turned
right instead of left at the end of a walkway
and fell with silent speed into the chimney which conducted smoke
from the ten coke-fuelled furnaces driving the entire operation,
and was hauled out later as the day's ashes
and buried in the last corner of the orchard remaining
in the hope that, despite the depredations of industry,
a small corner of rural England would revive,
and possibly even give rise to a new breed of Cox's Spiffin.

So it is, that these days, as we go about our business,
whether in China or the furthest tip of the South American
    continent,
our lives are reshuffled in a glum valley-fold of Herefordshire
by a Moloch which has not stopped since eighteen sixty-seven,
although a conversion from solid to more environmentally
    friendly fuel
was made in nineteen seventy-four, and the whole enterprise
costs you, me and the country absolutely nothing, being
a model of economics in a state of free-fall whose
inexplicable self-regulation is a cause for wonder and puzzlement,
and the workers who tend its operation,
and the cheerful postcards from the absentee landlord who has
    leased out the terrain,
and the countless coach parties of visitors who solemnly file past it,
and the building of new roads which lead to and from it,
and the installation of ever more complex early-warning systems –

all this is futile, as the archaic apparatus is, after all,
a self-fuelling, coke-and-steam-propelled *perpetuum mobile*,
that is to say, it is impossible for anyone to modernise or repair it,
or invest in it, or inspect it, or even install child-proofing,
because what will happen will uselessly happen
through an unspeakable law of mechanics that is not in the
    textbooks,
and to install child-proofing is to guarantee that boys on the roof
will fall through a skylight to the concrete floor two hundred feet
    below, so it is
best not to hasten the inevitable by doing anything about it, and
    quite honestly
'unspeakable' is the word one has to use because people
who visit the colossus do not speak, there is a severe hush
    everywhere
even as the thing itself clashes and hammers,
indeed, apart from those who go expressly to see it
(and then for the remainder of their lifetimes refrain from
    speaking of it)
there is what one might call a conspiracy of not-talking-about-it,
so that even maps do not include the orchard's location
and neither Jacques le Sourd nor Hamish McPosset are mentioned
in *Encyclopaedia Britannica* or any other work of reference,
and there are no signposts along the main road out of Worcester,
although the bus drivers somehow know the way.

Yet, at home, standing in a garden in the silence of a summer night,
smelling the heavy, brackish, heart-leeching perfume
that rises from an accidentally disturbed bush of *I-Forget-the-Name*,
and looking up into the blackness across which Mavis Doolittle's
    comet
is making its millennial way towards the end of the universe,
and smoking, perhaps, one of your Ataturk cigarettes,
drawing gentle puffs of piratical fume deep into your poor lungs,
you will look back on your life and see how everything
    went wrong,

but subtly, faintly, not in any major way you could claim sympathy
    for,
as if you had once turned a corner too late to see the one you love
turn a corner ahead of you, so that you just went on not having
    seen her,
and although there is a saying: *what you can't see, can't see you either*,
this is actually a popular adage I would like to take the opportunity
    here
of passionately denouncing as a damned fallacy, a lie, an imposture,
because however quickly gone it may be,
the moment of not being seen is worth having, and I would like
to suggest, therefore, that you close your eyes
and imagine for yourself the infernally clanking locomotive,
and then open your eyes again, exhale gently, a microsecond closer
    to death,
and see the *Liebesweh*, the *Ripefrock*, the *Spot-on-the-Lung*, the
    Odorendrum
whose scent fills the night air and dims the stars and makes your
    heart slow
and ravishes you upon your walk around the garden
before you finally enter the house for a nightcap
of that faintly resinous Mixed Blessing you like so much
and a slice of Trembling Bulldog before bed.

PACKAGE DEAL

The dawn rose over the celebrated optical illusion.
Breakfast was inedible. It drew laughs.
There was a heavy twelve-sided coin with a hole in it
you couldn't use to tip the staff.

I went on the excursion to the Holy Tooth.
So many hairpin bends, the driver stoned or pissed.
One night there was no food. A guest remarked:
'I think the tide is saying *Listen!*'

Queries and complaints were forwarded to the manager
when a pervasive stench recurred around one a.m.
We all enjoyed the visit to The Bay of Qualms, however.
The Holy Sandcastle was trampled on by children.

Beside the fissured torso of Jesus,
someone placed candles.
'*Look!*' the great writer had written. At an exhibition
of his work, I bought a pair of sandals.

In the tall dark house of his exile,
T-shirts with his face on was what they wore.
I proffered the famous coin to the toilet attendant
who hurled it to the floor.

The writer's message did not go unread.
There was a 'Listen!' café, and a 'Look!' hotel.
The ground shook, and we all thought 'Eruption!',
remembering the sulphur smell.

'Come back!' cried the president of the island.
He was a man to whom culture mattered.
You sensed that. A bridge which shortened everyone's journey
was not on the map.

The airstrip had a volcano at one end, an ocean
at the other. The stewardess was sombrely attired.
I recall the effort of her smile.
During take off, the engines backfired.

But the beaches were lovely

HOT FIVE

'Gentlemen, the wax is hot and you may play.'
The clarinet swoops, the guitarist, with a fan of fingers,
                                    plays a chord,
cornet and trombone start a dirty quarrel
about which way to play the melody.

The leading hornman's first arpeggio
ravishes the scale, then with full vibrato
                                    skies a note
and holds it. The critic, taking pulse, feels
his pressure start a heady rise.

The trombone burps and blathers,
seesaws fatly, riding up
                like some stout citizen
loose inside an urchin's playground,
then down.

The clarinet's a seagull
following a ferry. Poised upon an updraught,
                                    it floats astern,
then wheels between the smokestacks,
crying out.

They play with a bottle of Miss Urzey's gin
open on the table. The guitarist,
                        with his legs crossed,
is leaning over his instrument. It looks
as if he's pulling something from his entrails.

The critic notes they've made it up —
or most of it — as they progress. He takes
                            a fluffed note

for 'the drastic nature of an inspiration'.
A collision on that fill-in — it sends

'a frisson of delight along your leg' the way
perfection never could. A chair in the studio
                                    falls over, faithfully recorded.
The main man soars across its bump. Somebody
is laughing, shouting, as the next solo ignites.

Twenty-eight years later, in an attic, a boy
winds the handle of an ancient gramophone,
                            opens wide its loudness doors
and puts a fat brass needle in the pick-up
(for the full impact of modern sound reproduction).

'What is the source of this music's power?
Social repression? Naïveté? Or does it just express
                                    the joy of being alive?'
The critic is genuinely puzzled. He writes: 'perhaps
it was a moment when art and popularity coincided.'

In the attic, trombone, clarinet and cornet
storm towards the end of their three minutes:
                                    'the final *rapprochement*
of that polyphonic ride-out lifts us into a new dimension.'
Quite. And the needle scratches on the playout groove.